ROBIN HOOD™

PRINCE OF THIEVES

ROBIN HOOD™
PRINCE OF THIEVES

THE OFFICIAL MOVIE BOOK

GARTH PEARCE

MALLARD
PRESS

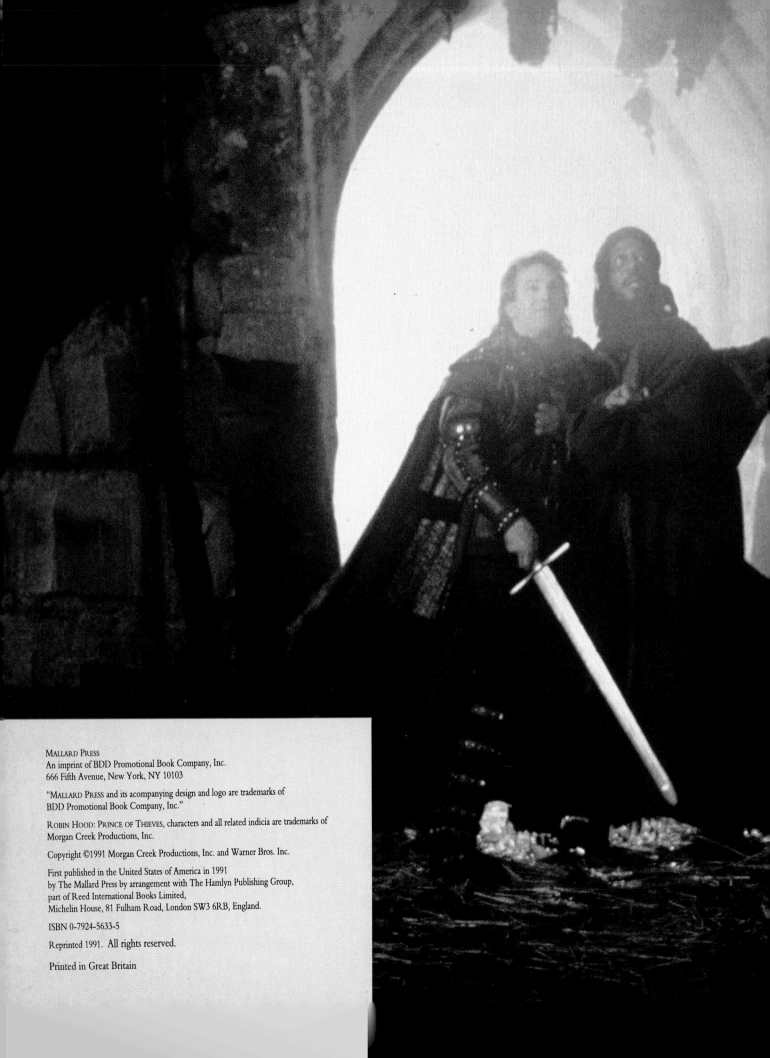

MALLARD PRESS
An imprint of BDD Promotional Book Company, Inc.
666 Fifth Avenue, New York, NY 10103

"MALLARD PRESS and its acompanying design and logo are trademarks of
BDD Promotional Book Company, Inc."

ROBIN HOOD: PRINCE OF THIEVES, characters and all related indicia are trademarks of
Morgan Creek Productions, Inc.

Copyright ©1991 Morgan Creek Productions, Inc. and Warner Bros. Inc.

First published in the United States of America in 1991
by The Mallard Press by arrangement with The Hamlyn Publishing Group,
part of Reed International Books Limited,
Michelin House, 81 Fulham Road, London SW3 6RB, England.

ISBN 0-7924-5633-5

Reprinted 1991. All rights reserved.

Printed in Great Britain

Contents

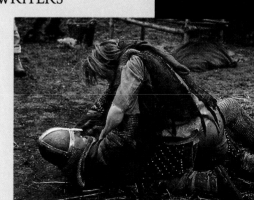

Foreword

We all need heroes. People have always wanted heroes. The ancients had their Achilles, Hercules, and Samson. The moderns have their Superman and Batman. Folk heroes pervade every culture - Canada has its Paul Bunyan, America its Davey Crockett, Switzerland its William Tell. These characters have become the staples of popular fiction in all its evolving forms and recurring characters in childhood games. If you grew up in England, as we did, the chances are you spent a lot of your early years pretending you were in Sherwood Forest with a bow and arrow.

In the 20th Century, Robin Hood may have become the world champion folk hero. Nobody has had more movies made about him and in more languages. He has been played by Douglas Fairbanks Sr., Errol Flynn and Sean Connery. Every journalist and visitor touring the Morgan Creek film set recounted how popular Robin Hood is in their own country, even in Asia, Africa, and South America. What is it about this fellow? Is it his prowess as an archer? His championing of the poor? His romantic life in the forest? His fight for right against might? Maybe it's the popular supporting cast of characters - no other folk hero comes complete with his own built-in love interest, his own companions, and villains.

Whatever the reasons for Robin Hood's popularity, we found we couldn't resist putting another arrow in his quiver. We wanted today's generation to be inspired by a fresh incarnation of the Sherwood rebel. However, anytime you fool around with everyone's favourite hero, you run a big risk. While you want to make him new, fresh and different, you better not make him *too* different. You want to give them Maid Marian, Little John, Friar Tuck and the evil Sheriff of Nottingham. You also want to add some new characters, some fresh twists and some real surprises! We took up the challenge, and it was fun. We hope you enjoy our version as much as we enjoyed creating it. Who knows? Maybe some of you will be bringing us the next Robin Hood film(s) of the 21st Century. In the meantime, see you all in Sherwood Forest.

John Watson and Pen Densham
PRODUCERS AND SCREENWRITERS

Robin Hood
THE MYTH AND THE MOVIES

"*About this time arose*
from the dispossessed and banished
that famous Robert [sic] Hood
and Little John with their companions.
They lived as outlaws among
the woodlands and thickets."

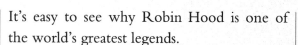

It's easy to see why Robin Hood is one of the world's greatest legends.

A son of nobility, who lives with a group of friends in the forest, robbing the rich to feed the poor. What could be more appealing?

So did Robin really exist? Cynics say he did not; that it is just a medieval fairy tale which has been exaggerated over the years. They point to the lack of absolute proof of *who* he was to back them up.

But historians greatly outnumber the debunkers. There are too many documents from the 13th Century which point to a real-life character. It is only his exploits that have been exaggerated - not his existence.

The first documented proof of the existence of Robin Hood is in what were called the County "Pipe Rolls" of Yorkshire (in the north of England) in 1230. This was an Exchequer's guide to each county on accounts and taxes. In a handwritten scroll - in Latin, as all documents in England were then - reference is made to "Robertus Hood, Fugitivus" (Robin Hood - fugitive). Robin was a nickname for Robert, which was a common name in the English

RIGHT: Douglas Fairbanks Sr. in the first Robin Hood for United Artists (1922). BELOW: A swashbuckling Errol Flynn with Olivia de Havilland as Marian, in THE ADVENTURES OF ROBIN HOOD for Warner Bros. (1938).

The Adventures of ROBIN HOOD

ERROL FLYNN
OLIVIA de HAVILLAND
BASIL RATHBONE
CLAUDE RAINS

Middle Ages. Since the old Sherwood Forest spread northwards and overlapped into deeply wooded areas of South Yorkshire at that time, the simple conjecture is that Robin was doing what we know him for - escaping the taxman by living in the forest.

By the 1300s, Robin Hood had become a celebrity. In 1341 John Fordun, the Canon of Aberdeen, Scotland who made regular excursions to England to collect material for his histories, pinpointed Robin's adventures to around 1266.

"About this time," he wrote, "arose from the dispossessed and banished that famous Robert (*sic*) Hood and Little John with their companions. They lived as outlaws among the woodlands and thickets, of whom the common people are so extravagantly fond of celebrating in tragedy and comedy; and the ballads concerning who, sung by jesters and minstrels, delight them above all others." Minstrels were the news-carriers of their day. They would travel from village to village, mixing current events with references to past history. It seems that news of Robin's exploits travelled with them for the best part of 150 years before an increasing number of versions of the story made it into print.

The theme of the free but persecuted outlaw enjoying forbidden hunting in the forest and outwitting the forces of law and order captured the mood of the country. Most of the English population were poor. It was a time of serfdom and landed gentry. Simmering discontent against the monied, land-owning ruling class resulted in The Peasant's Revolt of 1381. In the stories and ballads, Little John became the most established companion of Robin. The most frequent enemy is the Sheriff of Nottingham. Historians all have their theories.

Author Jim Lees, former President of The

John Derek as Robin in Columbia's THE ROGUES OF SHERWOOD FOREST (1950).

Robin Hood Society, based in Nottingham, is regarded as Britain's greatest living expert. He has devoted 30 years virtual non-stop research to the subject, culminating in books like *The Quest For Robin Hood*. He's now convinced that Robin was a 13th Century Knight Errant called Robert de Kyme, living between 1210 and 1278. His adventures took him from the Welsh borders, through Shropshire, Staffordshire and Derbyshire to Nottingham, where the legend took root.

Lees has also pointed out that Friar Tuck had no place in the early ballads. A "Frere Tucke" appeared in a commission dated 1429, when he was "pardoned for all crimes." The name of "Frere Tuck" then became a regular alias among criminals. But he does not make an entry into the official Robin Hood story until *Robin Hood's Golden Prize* of 1620.

It's the same with Maid Marian. A late entry: this time in Alexander Barclay's *Eclogues*, published in 1508. The belief is that it had become fashionable to mime Robin

Hood stories at the May Day festival and he needed a love interest. Marian was added merely to be in keeping with May

So this is how things have been for nearly 800 years, characters and bits of the story being added, perhaps to suit convention or the needs of the time. Hollywood, ever the mother of invention, has simply taken its lead from history and played to the audience. When Robin Hood made his big-budget debut in 1922, with Douglas Fairbanks Sr., the world was recovering from a very bloody war. It needed cheering up. Result: the biggest set in the history of Hollywood, a huge three million dollar budget and what was described as a "rollicking" film.

When Warner Bros. came forth with their own version in 1938, *The Adventures of Robin Hood*, it was a vehicle for their biggest stars - with Errol Flynn as Robin and Olivia de Havilland as Marian - to show what they could do. Flynn was in magnificent swashbuckling form. He fought duels, shot arrows, humiliated the Sheriff and rescued women, all for the then huge sum of $2,000 a week.

There was an amazing twist in the 1950s: would Robin escape the McCarthy ban in America on communists? He did, of course. Just to make sure America would remember him a new series was winging its way to TV screens across the nation. The English actor Richard Greene appeared in 165 half-hour episodes which many remember as their introduction to Robin as a screen hero.

Greene followed through in 1960 with a full-length British film version, incidentally called *Sword of Sherwood Forest*, which was distributed by Columbia.

We waited 16 years for another serious stab at it, again from Columbia, in the shape of *Robin and Marian* (1976) with the evergreen Sean Connery as a mature Robin and

Audrey Hepburn as Marian. It was a more realistic look at medieval life, without glamour. The cast was packed with well-known actors, including Denholm Elliott, Nicol Williamson, Richard Harris and Ian Holm, but received mixed reviews.

Ironically, it was Sean's son Jason who set hearts fluttering in the role in 1985. His British TV version, called *Robin of Sherwood*, in which he took over from actor Michael Praed, established him as a rising star at the age of just 21.

But those are some of the

ABOVE: Don Taylor in MEN OF SHERWOOD FOREST (1954). RIGHT: A poster of Warner Bros.' ROBIN AND THE SEVEN HOODS (1964) with Frank Sinatra, Dean Martin, Bing Crosby and Sammy Davis Jr.

ABOVE: Richard Greene as the archetypal Robin Hood in Columbia's SWORD OF SHERWOOD FOREST (1960). RIGHT: Sean Connery as an older Robin in ROBIN AND MARIAN (1976).

highlights. What other versions have there been in between? *Robin Hood of El Dorado* (1936) turned Warner Baxter into a western version of the outlaw from Sherwood Forest; *Robin Hood of Texas* (1947) followed a similar theme with Gene Autry. What with *Robin Hood of the Pecos* (Gabby Hayes, 1941), *Robin Hood of the Range* (Charles Starrett, 1943) and

Robin Hood of Monterey (Gilbert Roland, 1947), Robin had quite a rough ride of it during the 1940s.

But *Rogues of Sherwood Forest* in 1950 with John Derek in the title role was reasonably satisfactory. The plot, with the son of Robin Hood helping the barons to force the signing of Magna Carta, took great liberties with history. But what plot doesn't?

The Story of Robin Hood and His Merrie Men (1952) delivered a softer, Walt Disney telling of the tale, with Richard Todd smartly dressed in green and sporting an early Fifties haircut.

Men of Sherwood Forest, another British effort of 1954 with Don Taylor as Robin, had him freeing King Richard from bondage in Jerusalem.

The Walt Disney Studios were to have another go in 1973 - this time with a full-length animated version with a fox called *Robin Hood*. All cartoons of Robin up to that time had been "shorts." Another animated version came a year later: *Robin Hood, The Invincible Archer*.

Robin is far from being exclusively British - or American - either. *Robin Hood and the Pirates* (1963) was an Italian version. Even the Russians got in on the act in 1976 with *Robin Hood*, starring their own Boris Khmielnitski.

So what with comic versions, with the likes of *Robin and the Seven Hoods* (Frank Sinatra, 1964) and a TV film *The Zany Adventures of Robin Hood* (George Segal, 1984), where does that leave poor Robin? The truth is, in an extremely strong position. Despite differing verdicts from film critics around the world, Robin Hood has never flopped at the box office.

And *Robin Hood: Prince of Thieves* looks set to be his greatest screen success yet.

The Prince of Thieves

Robin of Locksley and his friends, including Azeem, Will Scarlett, Little John, and Friar Tuck, band together as outlaws in the depths of Sherwood Forest.

Kevin Costner

Kevin Costner's emergence from an actor to superstar has been swift and surprising, even by Hollywood standards. At the start of the 1980s, he was a theatre stage manager, still hoping he would eventually be able to support wife Cindy on income from acting. Now he commands millions of dollars a movie and at 35 has established an enviable reputation as both actor and director.

His last movie, the award-winning *Dances with Wolves* (1990), had High Risk stamped all over it. It not only marked his directorial debut, but the subject matter - a three-hour Western in which his American cavalry officer befriends the Sioux Indians - hardly looked set to excite much interest. But he turned an unlikely story into box office gold, receiving the Golden Globe awards for best film and best director, and twelve Academy Award nominations. Only one other film, *Who's Afraid of Virginia Wolf* (1966) received more (thirteen). This critical acclaim has meant that his excursion even further back into history with *Robin Hood: Prince of Thieves* has aroused great expectations.

> *"If acting is in your soul, you can't give it up. Some people are born to it. That's the way I felt."* KEVIN COSTNER

But Costner, whose film acting debut in *Night Shift* (1982) came only nine years ago, has always risen on the back of unfashionable choices. Only in retrospect does he seem to have chosen carefully and with an almost uncanny knack of knowing what the public wants.

In *No Way Out*, a 1987 re-make of *The Big Clock* (1948) about a Pentagon officer who is convinced his boss is guilty of murder, he is remembered for a hot love scene in the back of a car

Kevin Costner

with the controversial Sean Young. *The Untouchables* (1987) quickly followed. Would there be an audience for a new update on the 1920s crime-buster Elliott Ness? Yes, there was. Costner's boyish, clean-cut good looks carried the role perfectly. With Sean Connery cast as an ageing beat cop who could act as a brake on his more impetuous decisions, the film worked as a perfect coupling for the box office.

In *Bull Durham* (1989), a straightforward tale of a baseball hero, co-starring Susan Sarandon as his older lover, any remaining doubters of his instant sex appeal were hit right out of the ball park. Then came *Field of Dreams* (1989). This was the oddest choice and one that looked ludicrous on paper: a struggling farmer who is moved to build a baseball field which is visited by ghosts of former baseball giants. But the film, brilliantly scripted and acted, struck a chord with audiences. Many were reduced to tears by the poignant sub-plot based on childhood criticism of a father, who later puts in an appearance as a vigorous young man.

Costner's tastes in films - strong characterization, action and a story that will appeal to cinema audiences across the world - goes back to childhood. He lived with parents and brother Danny, five years his senior, in the working class area of Compton, California.

When brother Danny was drafted and sent to Vietnam in 1968, Kevin at nearly 13 started taking notes of his experiences. Recalls Danny: "He told me he wanted to write about the white working-class experience in the Vietnam War. I was really surprised that he was interested."

Both feet were always firmly on the ground. At Villa Park High School in Orange County, California, he is remembered as an average student - but a fanatical sportsman. Ironically, he was of small to average height during school; by the time he left Fullerton University he was almost 6 feet 1 inch. He graduated in 1978 with an honours degree in business studies - and married Cindy the same year. He had no regular job and very few prospects.

Although he had started acting classes at college for four nights a week, he could not get a full-time job. Instead, he worked in a variety of ways to get money.

"I worked on fishing boats as a deckhand, drove trucks, worked in ice-houses and was a carpenter for a time," he recalls. "I was also a tour guide on the buses up to San Francisco, pointing out the tourist spots from Los Angeles on Pacific Coast Highway. But I finally decided that I was going to be an actor, because if I was not going to make the grade and take out trash it might as well be movie trash. If acting is in your soul, you can't give it up. Some people are born to it. That's the way I felt."

Wife Cindy, with whom he has now had three children - Annie, six, Lily, four, and two-year-old Joe - has seen it all. While her husband struggled to find acting work, she worked as part of the groundstaff of Delta Airlines in Los Angeles.

ABOVE: Robin mourns the death of his father Lord of Locksley, after burying him.
RIGHT: Guy of Gisborne is caught trespassing on Robin's land.
BELOW: Robin and Will Scarlett (Christian Slater) at the camp.

"Is it not a greater crime to starve a family? Now if you would be so kind as to give me your name, sir, before I run you through."

"I am a rich man's son.
But today I am as poor as any of you.
And when I killed the Sheriff's men,
I too became an outlaw..."
Thus a legend was born.

BELOW: Maid Marian
(Mary Elizabeth
Mastrantonio) and Robin
rendezvous in his camp
deep in the heart
of Sherwood Forest.

Kevin Costner portrays the legendary hero Robin Hood with the perfect blend of style, humour, and courage.

Kevin Costner
AS ROBIN HOOD

What won Kevin Costner over to the story of *Robin Hood: Prince of Thieves* was the chance of non-stop action. He's one of only a handful of Hollywood actors who relishes a real fight. Other cast members watched in surprise at his obvious enjoyment at riding horses at the gallop, swinging from trees at great heights and risking injury in sword battles or hand-to-hand blows with six-foot staffs.

For a man who is affable and relaxed, he takes on a hard edge when involved in action: "I am physical in my acting," he agrees. "I consider that it's part of what I have to offer. I have always been a fairly fit, sporting guy. I did all the traditional American sports: baseball, basketball, American football. So the chance of shooting bows and

> "Kevin Costner is a great romantic figure, the camera loves him, and audiences clearly love him" KEVIN REYNOLDS

Kevin Costner as Robin Hood

arrows and fighting with staves and swords is terrific. It is like being in a sports situation every day. There is a chance to use one of these weapons and try and reach perfection."

Another reason that Costner opted for this Robin Hood movie is that it was being directed by old friend Kevin Reynolds, who directed him in a 1984 film, *Fandango*.

"Kevin Reynolds knows my capabilities as much as anyone," Kevin Costner says. "We have our combative days, but know that our arguments are about the film itself and not other things."

Costner's own film memories of Robin Hood centre on the 1938 version, *The Adventures Of Robin Hood*, starring Errol Flynn in his famous green tights. "By the time I was watching that film on TV it must have been around 20 to 25 years old," he says. "But it was still terrific."

Word was obviously out that Costner would make a classic Robin. At one point there were three separate films planned about the outlaw – and Kevin was offered the lot. "I honestly don't know why that was," he reflects with a smile. "Do I look like Robin Hood? But I was happy and knew I could have a lot of fun with a film like this.

"With this script, his spirit is challenged right from the start. He's been to the Crusades, was captured but then manages to escape prison. So that immediately added a lot of weight and colour to the way I play him. I do not want to take the spirit away from him, but he is clearly a world traveller. He is not someone who has lived only in Sherwood Forest with a narrow view." Costner continues: "He's seen real death and gore and the true face of the

ABOVE: Robin and Azeem (Morgan Freeman) develop a strong bond of friendship. BELOW: Action man Robin Hood, bow at the ready, races to help his friends in the battle to save their camp.

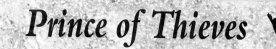

> *"He is an excellent horse rider – a better rider than I am, in fact."* SIMON CRANE: STUNT DOUBLE

Crusades. He was captured and had the time to reflect on his father's words... 'It is a vanity to force another man to your religion.' Robin escapes and returns to England, but it's too late... so the scene is set for Robin to right the wrongs.

"The result is that I can imagine how the man feels. We are not offering a repeat of the old Robin Hood story or an outlaw who has become just a parody of the legend."

He was also going to deliver a Robin Hood in record time. The race was on with rival Robin scripts to be first into production. "The director Kevin Reynolds was willing to start with just over a couple of months of preparation, whereas nobody else would touch a film like this unless they had five months prep," says Costner. "But that is typical of Kevin. It's a pretty big statement, but I believe Kevin Reynolds will be one of our greatest American directors in the next ten to 15 years."

The combination of the two Kevins seemed to steamroller the film through, with both energy and conviction, in a style which Robin himself would have been proud: "We want to capture solid excitement from start to finish," Costner says.

Azeem

Azeem is a brand new character introduced to the Robin Hood legend. "What I like most about the character is his dry humour," says Freeman. "Kevin is playing Robin as a young guy with a very physical outlook on life. I act as a restraining force. In fact, Azeem has a very sophisticated scientific knowledge and he brings this - Caesarean births and telescopes - to the people of Sherwood Forest and can hardly believe how backward the woodsmen really are."

Azeem first meets Robin in the filth of a Middle East prison. During a dramatic escape, Robin saves his life. Azeem, true to Moorish tradition, feels bound to stay with Robin until he has a chance to properly repay him by saving *his* life.

MORGAN FREEMAN was pleasantly surprised to be offered the all-action role of Azeem, the intellectual Moor who becomes Robin's right-hand man. "After playing the aging chauffeur in *Driving Miss Daisy* [1990], I had lots of offers to play old men," he says, with a smile. "Despite my success, casting directors in Hollywood don't have too much imagination."

Far from being an old man, Morgan, 53, is exceptionally fit. He worked out in a gymnasium at Shepperton Studios for at least half-an-hour each day and stunt men were constantly staggered at his capabilities.

"He feels he may as well hitch his wagon to a young go-getter like Robin," says Morgan. "He seldom offers advice, but is always there making observations. Robin and the men have the choice of either ignoring him - or acting on what Azeem thinks."

Morgan Freeman was particularly popular during filming. His laid-back, gentlemanly approach to work and the film crew brought him much admiration. He has the same approach to his own life with his wife Myrna: "We have an apartment in New York - and a boat in the Caribbean where

LEFT: Morgan Freeman plays Azeem, the Moor who helps Robin eacape from the dungeons. RIGHT: Azeem tries to fend off Mortianna, the witch, in Nottingham Castle. BELOW: Azeem is a scientist as well as a warrior. Here he assembles a primitive but effective telescope.

advice and the same still applies." Since then, of course, Hollywood has indeed sent for Morgan Freeman, after he established a top Broadway theatre reputation. The result has been Best Actor Oscar nominations for *Driving Miss Daisy* and *Street Smart* (1990), plus top roles in films like *Clean and Sober* (1989) and *Glory* (1990).

we live much of the time," he reports. "We have an address, but *no 'phones*. My agent does not get in touch with me...I 'phone him. I prefer it that way. I bought the boat from the proceeds of *Lean On Me* [1988] a couple of years ago and we decided just to live. It is a good policy.

"I remember back in 1973 when there was an exodus of black actors from New York to Hollywood, I was wondering whether I should follow. My agent said: 'No - stay where you are. If Hollywood is interested, it will send for you.' It was good

"But if I lived there, I would only be striving to get the right car and live in the right neighbourhood," he reasons. "As I grew up in Mississippi, I love the open country and getting away from it all. In the Caribbean the sea is still clean and the local islanders are concerned with their environment. I enjoy just cruising around, hanging out with friends and doing lots of nothing."

He brought that attitude to all the locations in the frantically-paced *Robin Hood Prince of Thieves*: "I would never get a breakdown," he smiled. "From the moment I stop acting in front of the cameras, I can relax. I am so happy when I am working. I feel as if I'm just working through life's ambitions and dreams."

> "Morgan is probably the fittest actor on this set. He works out each day and is like a powerhouse."
> PAUL WESTON
> STUNT CO-ORDINATOR

Maid Marian

> **"Once I realized that this Maid Marian has plenty of guts I was into the part."**

opposite Kevin Kline in *The January Man* (1989) and in the underwater drama *The Abyss* (1990), with Ed Harris, which grabbed the headlines.

But Mary's tumbling dark hair and feisty Italian background was thought to be perfect for the determined Maid Marian, who is more than a match for Robin Hood himself.

The fact she had not met Kevin Costner before did not bother her in the slightest: "I am not one of those actresses who believe you should spend a week in each other's company, just to get to know the other person," she says.

"Acting is about just getting on with doing it. The story was new – Robin Hood to me was just Errol Flynn in tights - so there was much to learn and absorb. I think it is far better to just turn up and start work. Meetings with actors beforehand is just like a blind date. Once I realized that this Maid Marian has plenty of guts I was into the part. She is not just someone to hang on the arm of Robin, so I thought: 'Count me in.' "

The part also gave Mary Elizabeth a

On the face of it, MARY ELIZABETH MASTRANTONIO was an unlikely choice as Maid Marian. Until *Robin Hood*, Mary was known for roles which were more street-sharp than Sherwood.

She impressed audiences and critics alike as Tom Cruise's very savvy girlfriend in the Oscar-winning film *The Color of Money* (1986). Before that, she was with Al Pacino in *Scarface* (1983); later came the appearance

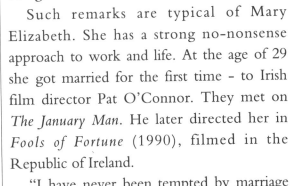

chance to observe that the British class system had changed little in 800 years between the real Robin Hood and the 1990s.

"I was one of six daughters of a foundry-man from Oak Park, Illinois," she says. "But no-one knows that fact when I open my mouth. England is far more class conscious. It matters how you speak and which area you live in. And with England's sense of history, people often say: 'Oh, I was born at the wrong time.' I say: 'Look at yourself. You'd have been probably scrubbing floors if you lived a few hundred years ago - not sitting around in corsets being waited on.' "

Such remarks are typical of Mary Elizabeth. She has a strong no-nonsense approach to work and life. At the age of 29 she got married for the first time - to Irish film director Pat O'Connor. They met on *The January Man*. He later directed her in *Fools of Fortune* (1990), filmed in the Republic of Ireland.

"I have never been tempted by marriage until now," says Mary Elizabeth. "I have had a few serious relationships, but marriage is something that had never occurred to me. Perhaps Maid Marian has got to me more than I care to admit!"

Marian takes her leave of Robin and his outlaws in the forest (ABOVE), and with the Sheriff of Nottingham at their hurried wedding ceremony in the Chapel (LEFT).

Will Scarlett

> *"Will was obviously a bit of wild child, too, and that comes over well. He's had to grow up fast."*

CHRISTIAN SLATER is a 21-year-old who has become super-hot in the wake of contemporary movies like *Heathers* (1989), *Young Guns II* (1990) and *Pump Up the Volume* (1990).

But his film career has come full circle in just six years. He first made an impact as Sean Connery's apprentice in the medieval classic *The Name of the Rose* (1986) when he was just 15. Now, he is back in the 12th Century once more as the rebellious Will Scarlett.

"Several things were put into the script after I was cast," he reveals. "For instance, the fact that Robin Hood really screwed up my life when I was younger. His father dated my mother and I was the result. I came forth into the world as Robin's half-brother. There is one point in the film when I have to tell Robin the truth. So it adds an edge to the whole movie for me. Will was obviously

a bit of a wild child, too, and that comes over well. He's had to grow up fast."

The same could be said of Christian Slater. He was a child actor, though he recalls that his casting agent mother was "not thrilled" that he wanted to go in to acting. "She sees actors all the time and knows how tough it is," he says. "But once she saw how much I was enjoying myself, she relaxed."

Christian has also been tempted to fall in to the trap of getting too much, too soon. "I was on a self-destructive path for God knows what reason," he says. "I have checked myself and now move forward at one day at a time. I think to myself: 'Hey - don't throw it all away.' "

Part of it, he admits, is caused by genuine nerves at working with some of the major stars: "One of the things I wish I'd have done with Sean was to go up to him on the first day of shooting *Name Of The Rose* and tell him how nervous I was," he now says. "With Morgan Freeman (Azeem) on this one, I went up and said: 'I am incredibly star-struck. I am a big fan of yours. I might have a difficult time in chatting it up with you.' Morgan was very understanding and put his arms around me. I have had no trouble with Morgan at all and have learned to relax on set."

> **"He's just a big guy who happens to be the toughest of the ones in the forest until Robin comes along..."**

Little John

The only time NICK BRIMBLE looks fierce is when he's wielding a heavy quarterstaff on the heads of his enemies, as Little John. Away from the role, Brimble is a gentle giant of a man. He may be 6 feet 4 inches tall with the strength to kick his way through a barn door, but there was always a genial smile and pleasant conversation between his action shots.

There is a ready acceptance that with his build and expression in front of the camera, he is always going to be in line for work as heavies or villains.

"I was hoping originally to be playing Guy Of Gisborne," he admits. "I thought it would be a more interesting role. The trouble with being pitched for Little John was that I felt he would be a giant with not too much to say. Yet the director Kevin Reynolds assured me there was more to it than that! He had the character of John Little in mind - a big man, but not grotesque, who has a wife and lots of children. He lives in a village and only takes to the woods because of the treatment villagers are receiving from the Sheriff of Nottingham.

"He's just a big guy who happens to be

the toughest of the ones in the forest - until Robin Hood comes along. Robin becomes John's hero after that and he does not resent him in any way. Little John is a very simple man with not a great intellect. But he has a good heart."

Bristol-born Brimble is academically highly qualified. He received a Bachelor of Arts degree in philosophy and a Masters degree in English literature at Sussex University; he then taught at the University of Baghdad before returning to the United Kingdom to teach English and drama.

Only then did he try his hand at acting, receiving no formal training: "I took a job with the Marlowe Theatre in Canterbury, Kent for £10 ($19) a week, running workshops for kids," he recalls. "I was more excited at being involved in a theatre than anything I'd done before. So I was hooked."

There followed years of being mostly a theatre actor in England at Exeter's Northcott, Liverpool's Everyman and the Ipswich Theatre. He was also given leading roles at the National Theatre, London and the Royal Shakespeare Theatre.

His film debut came in a Hammer Horror movie called *Lust For A Vampire* (1970) and regular British TV work followed. In his last film he had the monster's role in Roger Corman's *Frankenstein Unbound* (1991), starring John Hurt and Bridget Fonda.

"I love movies and like being in them," says Nick. "But I have not had many chances apart from doing small parts. So there is a lot riding on Robin Hood for me. Also, Robin was a real hero to me as a kid.

"It's one of those stories, like King Arthur, that you grow up with. Living out in Sherwood Forest, fighting the horrible Normans, refusing to pay their taxes - and giving to the poor.

"It is a boy's dream come true."

Friar Tuck

MICHEAL McSHANE was originally rejected for the role as Friar Tuck: "I saw a casting agent in America and went down very badly indeed," he recalls. "I was out of that room in 20 minutes."

But when working in England on a comic television series called *Whose Line Is It Anyway*, he was given another chance by director Kevin Reynolds.

"He looked tired that day," says Micheal. "So I thought: I'll wake him up. I put plenty into the audition and made sure of getting it."

In fact, Californian McShane's life has shifted into overdrive since he moved from San Francisco for a year in England. He has two new situation comedies lined up for the British Channel 4 television station and a fast-growing cult following.

It's obvious that McShane loves his work. Even during those times on the film when he

Friar Tuck, Azeem and Robin turn to face the oncoming Celts at the beginning of the attack on their camp.

> "Tuck hopes that by
> the time he is 50 he will
> find some comfortable
> Abbey to live in. Then
> BOOM..."

no education, but is well trained in the science of making beer and wine. He is not good enough to be a vintner, so his role is that of a middle man. He gets the beer and trucks it off to the Abbey. They trust him because the monks know it is always going to be of good quality. Tuck hopes that by the time he is 50 he will find some comfortable abbey to live in. Then *boom*, he is interrupted.

"He is bothered by these thugs Robin Hood has with him. He is really angry and becomes brutal when he gets mad. He will hit out first and then ask: 'Well, what do you want?' He is a rat-ass fighter. He bites and claws people and gets stuck in. He does not lay off and start laughing. He is no Ho, Ho, Ho Friar who is in there for some comic relief."

McShane, 34, took a similar singular approach to his acting work after leaving school: "When I was 18 I joined the US Army for three years," he recalls. "In those days there was still what was called a GI Bill. The army paid your way in civilian life for two years after leaving. I thought I would spend three years learning about the military mind, having a few laughs and then use the

was not directly involved he would be sitting on set, brown friars' robes hitched up over his knees, as he watched other actors work. It typified Micheal's approach to the part and acting itself. He's an unconventional character who won't cut corners on detail.

"I did not want to play Friar Tuck as a fat Dudley Moore," he says. "No-one would want to be that drunk for that long. But I was unsure as to how I *did* want to play him. So, as a lapsed Catholic, I remembered what it was like in Rome. I would go and look at the priests and see how many different types there were. I wondered how Tuck would fit in. He is a Benedictine - so he is not an intellectual. He's a good-natured man with

OPPOSITE: *An archery contest between Robin and Wulf.* RIGHT: *Will Scarlett.* BELOW: *Tuck pulls his wagon into camp.* BOTTOM LEFT: *Marian learns of her brother's fate.* BOTTOM RIGHT: *Much (Jack Wild) and Bull (Daniel Peacock) spring a trap.*

GI Bill money to put myself through amateur theatres and learn acting."

For much of the time in the army he was based at Fort Knox, Kentucky, where the US gold is kept. But he did not find golden times ahead in acting. He struggled doing odd jobs to make up his money once his GI Bill finance ran out. Then, in 1980, he attended San Francisco State University to get a degree in Set Design and Acting. "It has been a struggle. But when I am on a film set like this one, I think it's worth it."

> "I want this brigand found!
> Slaughter their…livestock.
> I want Locksley's own people
> fighting to bring his head in."

The Sheriff
AND HIS HENCHMEN

> "I want this brigand found!
> Slaughter their…livestock.
> I want Locksley's own people
> fighting to bring his head in."

The Sheriff of Nottingham

suffer fools. He chooses his words carefully and they are ladled out as if he is not really happy talking about himself at all. On the offer on Robin Hood, for example, he says: "I was not particularly taken with the idea. I thought: 'What? Robin Hood - *again*?' "

But there was a change of heart once the script was in his hands: "I read it and thought of more potential for the Sheriff," he says. "I had been doing other things between *Die Hard* and this, so I thought it was okay to arch my eyebrow again in villainy."

He was with Kevin Kline in *The January Man* (1989) and with Tom Selleck in *Quigley Down Under* (1990). "Fortunately, I learned to ride a horse in *Quigley*, which was set in the Australian Outback," he reports. "I discovered later that all those scenes ended up on the cutting room floor. I was upset about that, until I got on to Robin Hood.

Actor ALAN RICKMAN brings a shudder of fear to the screen every time he makes his entrance as the Black Magic-worshipping Sheriff of Nottingham. Already, he has established himself with one of cinema's most memorable bad-guy performances as the gang boss in the action film *Die Hard* (1989).

In real life, though not thankfully having the edge of evil or nastiness he so readily brings to his roles, Alan Rickman does not

"I am supposed to be sitting on my horse on a ridge. On the day of the scene, director Kevin Reynolds comes up and says: 'You are okay on a horse, aren't you?' I then find that I am going to be riding down a slope on a nervy horse and I can only use one hand, because I am holding a sword in the other. That is the moment I thanked God for all those riding lessons a year before!"

ABOVE: The Sheriff watches his mercenaries destroy the woodsmen's camp.
BELOW: Entertaining a lady friend in the castle.

The Sheriff gently takes the intimidated girl's hand, draws it to his mouth as if to kiss it…bites down, making her scream.

He was also warming to his part when news came through of the all-star cast: "I was excited about Micheal McShane as Tuck, because I love *Whose Line Is It Anyway*," he says. "And what with Geraldine McEwan as Mortianna and Mary Elizabeth Mastrantonio, who I worked with in *The January Man*, I knew I was with some excellent people."

Alan also appreciated the energies of Kevin Costner: "Hollywood is such an unforgiving place that actors like Costner, Selleck and Kline do not stay at the top by accident," he says. "They are all very talented and bloody hard workers."

Alan Rickman is known mostly for his British stage work. But the transfer of *Les Liaisons Dangereuses* from London to Broadway, New York introduced him to the American audience. There were many who felt that he should have also got the film part in *Dangerous Liaisons* (1990), which went to John Malkovich; if Rickman feels any resentment now, he certainly does not show it. "I had absolutely no film background at all," he says flatly. "It was going to be a big risk."

Instead, he was given his key role in *Die*

Hard: "The producer, Joel Silver, came to see me in my dressing room in New York and gave me a very strange screen test. Someone came in with a hand-held video camera, probably to show Bruce Willis at a later stage, and I had to do one or two lines. I was hired because I was cheap. You have to be realistic."

But the role came at a perfect point: "After doing eight stage shows a week for three hours at a time, I was working in a warm climate, staying in a pleasant Hollywood house and doing only a page of dialogue a day. Films do have their advantages…"

Guy of Gisborne

When actor MICHAEL WINCOTT discusses his role as the cruel persecutor and occasional murderer of the poor, Guy of Gisborne, he wears a look of undisguised delight.

"It's terrific to play an out-and-out villain," Wincott says. "The villains are always so much more interesting to play - and this guy is a real son of a bitch. What is fascinating is that this guy is so solitary; so very alone. That is even more interesting than the evil aspect.

"I wish there was a way of showing more of Gisborne, but I am a realist. This movie is about Robin Hood and we don't want to confuse the central issue."

"What is fascinating is that this guy so solitary; so very alone. That is even more interesting than the evil aspect.'

But Guy will catch the eye. Wincott maximizes his character's dark side by wearing a costume of jet black and a constant, unblinking stare. Make-up supervisor Paul Engelen has also sculptured a savagely disfigured right ear, the result of a near-miss swordfight. Definitely a case of Gisborne looking like the bad Guy all right.

"I find something new about Gisborne on each day we film," says Michael. "But as one day is never the same as the last, I am not the person to tell you whether I'm getting it right all the time."

Was there any of the Robin Hood legend which was part of his own childhood? "No," says Michael. "I could not imagine anything about him that was part of my background, which was an urban environment. Anything that romantic came from a world in your head or just books. Also, in terms of the way it was depicted in films we had the Errol Flynn version and that was it."

He trained at one of America's most prestigious drama schools, Julliard. With more than 20 major stage credits to his name, his particular admiration of theatre actors led to a special friendship with Morgan Freeman.

"I went to see him in *The Taming of the Shrew* in New York and he was terrific, as always," he says. "He busted his ass in New York theatres for 22 years and there aren't many actors like that any more. Compared with that, films have advantages. Look at us, how lucky we are. Trailers and nice hotels. People to pamper you, guys asking if you want a coffee, all your needs catered for."

Mortianna's apothecary is a place of dread, inhabited by a woman who strikes fear into all those who see her. Shadows and strange glows rake the ancient walls. She uses blood, goose eggs and carved bones - called runes - to forecast the future and keeps burned or butchered animals all around her.

Mortianna is the Sheriff's secret guide in the fearsome art of Black Magic. She hands him warnings of problems in advance and urges that he deal most cruelly with any enemy. It is she who urges him to use Celt mercenaries to destroy Robin; she who insists that he marry Maid Marian.

Actress GERALDINE McEWAN, who had the task of injecting such deep evil into this heartless crone, could hardly wait to get her teeth into the part. "The moment I read the script, I thought: 'This is for me.' It is a wonderful role, and very different from anything I have ever done."

Geraldine is one of Britain's top actresses, with a string of classic parts going back to the Royal Shakespeare Theatre in the 1950s. She frequently co-starred with Olivier when he was Artistic Director of the National Theatre Company at the Old Vic, London and has won many Best Actress awards for work in the theatre.

"Mortianna is so extreme and unusual," she reports. "For a start, the make-up takes two hours. I have a mask of rubber to make my face look wrinkled, a bald cap, a wig with sparse white hair, a hump, opaque contact lenses, black teeth and brown fingernails.

"I find myself doing scenes with live snakes, rats and toads. In one, I had to hold offal in one hand, put it on a spear and feed a bat. In another, I stand over a table with a pig's head on which newts were crawling and hold up a live chicken by its legs in one hand and a sword in the other."

"The character is so ghastly," she says. "Normally, when I am filming for TV or appearing on stage I like to get lots of sleep so I can look good. But with Mortianna it did not matter at all if I looked awful in the morning. I knew that within minutes of my 7 a.m. start in make-up I was going to look *much* worse."

Mortianna

Then a wrinkled, monkey-like figure dances into view, wearing a necklace of chicken feet.

Robin, Azeem and Duncan (behind Azeem) flee Marian's estate, hotly pursued by Gisborne and his men.

And Action...

Escape from the Dungeon

The interrogator mocks: "How noble. As you wish. Cut off this one's hand as well!"

Robin is unchained. He defiantly holds his hand across the block. A jailer wraps a thong around his wrist. But as the scimitar arcs down, Robin pulls the jailer holding his hand so he receives the sword's blow. He then swings upwards, driving his fist into the executioner's throat. He grabs the sword as

Robin of Locksley (Kevin Costner) and Peter Dubois watch the torturers work in the fiery glow. Their appearance reeks of long imprisonment - white skin, knotted hair, dirty clothes.

It is The Holy Land in 1194, the third year of the Third Crusade, and both Robin and friend Peter's war looks over. An interrogator puts down his instruments and points towards the man he is torturing.

"He says you stole his bread," he says to Peter. "It's a lie," Peter replies. "I caught him stealing ours."

The victim of torture jabbers in Arabic and the interrogator orders Peter's hand to be cut off. He is released from iron collars around his wrists and ankles and hauled towards a chopping block. Peter is so frail he can hardly walk.

Robin intervenes: "No, I took the bread," he says. Peter replies: "That's not true." Robin turns to Peter: "They are not interested in truth. You are too weak. You would not live through it."

another jailer leaps at him. Robin slashes and the scimitar slices into the man's chest.

A warning is shouted: "Behind you!"

Robin turns to see another jailer swinging a giant axe. He shears the axe handle in two and runs through his attacker with the sword. As Peter frees himself of his remaining chains, Robin acknowledges the man who shouted the warning. He meets the eyes of an impassive Moor prisoner (Morgan Freeman), who is heavily chained.

"You speak English?" he observes. "The King's own," says the Moor. "Free me and I will show you a way out." "Why should we trust you?" asks Robin. "If you don't, you are dead men," comes the reply.

The door bursts open. More guards rush

in. Robin slashes the Moor's bindings and he leads them to a hidden door. Suddenly, they are outside in the fresh night air.

"God willing, we may now be safe," murmurs Robin. They do not see the silhouette of a guard on the prison wall. He fires his bow. An arrow pierces Peter's chest. Robin leads him under the wall for protection as the shout of alarm goes up around them. Robin tries to help Peter but the wound is mortal and he knows it. He shakes off Robin. The Moor looks at the arrow: "His wound is by the heart," he says. "We cannot save him."

Peter pulls an insignia ring from a hidden pouch in his clothes and thrusts it into Robin's hand. "Take this to my sister," he says. "Swear you will protect her for me." Robin reluctantly swears an allegiance. Peter then flings himself at the advancing soldiers, sweeping a sword wildly in front of him.

The Moor urges Robin: "Come, now. Make his sacrifice an act of honour." As they vanish into the night, Peter is swallowed up in a wave of enemy soldiers. Robin is safe. He and the Moor introduce themselves. The Moor, Azeem, pledges to be at Robin's side until he has a chance to save his life – as Robin had saved his.

And Robin, who feels that Azeem will be a big hindrance on his return to England, also knows that he has given himself a further responsibility with the pledge to Peter Dubois to take care of his sister: Maid Marian.

OPPOSITE LEFT: Robin of Locksley and his friend Peter Dubois languish in a Jerusalem dungeon. OPPOSITE RIGHT: A prisoner is tortured. ABOVE: Robin foils the guard's attempt to chop off his hand. BELOW: Robin and Peter escape with the aid of the mysterious Moor.

Robin Hood
Meets Little John

It is like no forest ever seen. Moss and lichen form a carpet. High above, hundred-foot high beeches and thousand-year-old oaks form a cathedral-like canopy.

Wide step-falls of a clear river cascade through a vale of trees and bracken. Robin Hood (Kevin Costner), Azeem (Morgan Freeman) and blind servant Duncan (Walter Sparrow) emerge from the lush undergrowth of the perimeter of Sherwood Forest.

Says Azeem: "In my dreams alone have I imagined such a place." Robin counters: "Well then, imagine a way to cross it."

Glancing upstream, he sees a potential bridge on top of the rushing falls. He starts picking his way across, using a stick for balance. Suddenly, a rope stretched across the river snakes out of the water, sweeping Robin's feet from under him.

Robin and Little John battle it out at the river crossing in Sherwood Forest. Although Little John has the upper hand to begin with, Robin finally succeeds in bettering his opponent.

As he splashes in the shallows, the bushes behind Azeem and Duncan come alive: shaggy, wild-eyed men armed with cudgels, scythes and hayforks come forward. One of them puts a spear to Azeem's back before he can move. Robin turns to try to stride to the other bank, but more men face him.

"Beg for mercy, rich man," calls Will

Robin Hood Meets Little John

Scarlett (Christian Slater).

Says Robin: "I beg of no man."

"This is our river. No-one crosses without paying tax."

"I will pay no tax. Besides, I have nothing but my cloak and sword."

The men part and a huge figure bellows: "A man who travels with two servants and claims he's without money is either a fool or a liar."

Will Scarlett emphasizes: "A liar!"

Robin looks at Azeem for assistance. His Moorish friend gives a helpless shrug of the shoulders, a spear still pointed at his back.

"Who are you?" he asks of the giant.

"John Little. Best man of the woods."

"Best man?" echoes Robin. "You lead this rabble?"

"I do."

He then sees the Locksley medallion around Robin's neck: "And if you want to cross Sherwood Forest it will cost you one gold medallion."

Robin shakes his head: "This is sacred to me."

"Sacred to us too," comes the retort. "That there will feed us for a blooming month."

Robin announces: "You will have to fight me for it."

John lunges for Robin's wrist and wrenches his sword free. He effortlessly bends it. Instead, he throws his gnarled quarter staff to Robin and is handed another by one of his men. John storms at Robin, who connects an instant blow on his foot. Robin also lands a couple to his ribs. But John chuckles with every swing.

With one mighty thrust, John drives the end of his staff into Robin's stomach. John then effortlessly turns Robin into the water. "A little wet behind the ears," he mocks.

Robin tries again, connecting several times. John loses balance and falls to his knees. Robin pole-vaults him with his staff and turns to face him. "It seems I've made it past the gate, John Little," he says. "Or should I call you Little John?"

With an angry roar, John comes at him again. Wood splinters from impact. Brute force pitched against agility. Robin's staff splits in two. "Swimming time again, ol' chum," says Little John, before hitting him again into the water, snatching the medallion from his neck as he does so.

Robin does not re-emerge. John waits. The men rush to the bank. There's no sign of him. "Shame," says John, biting the medallion to verify its gold content. "He were a brave 'un." As he strides from the bridge, Robin arcs up out of the water, grabs his ankles and heaves him into the river.

Suddenly, it's a different Little John. Flapping. Spluttering. Face full of panic. "I can't bloody swim," he shouts.

Robin thrusts Little John's head under again and again until he yields. Then Robin reveals this water is only waist deep. It marks the start of firm mutual admiration for each other's strengths. Robin is taken to a camp set up by Little John and Will Scarlett deep in the forest and begins to muster a fighting force to foil the Sheriff of Nottingham.

But the filming sequence, coming early in the location shoot, also set the pace and style of Kevin Costner. He insisted on doing the

action himself - much to the surprise of waiting stunt men and the actor who played Little John, Nick Brimble.

"If he was doing it, then so was I," Nick reports. "It meant carefully rehearsing the steps and swings of the staves. They are heavy and solid. One blow and it could put you out of the film. It was exhausting. I had to concentrate particularly hard on this action sequence. If I slipped up and accidentally landed a blow to Kevin's head, then he could well have been badly injured. That would have meant the entire production being put in jeopardy."

The hard-hitting sequence took four days to film in beautiful woodland around Aysgarth Falls in Yorkshire.

Top: *Robin is tripped up in the falls.* **Above:** *Little John threatens Robin.*

Attack on the Bullion Coach

Mounted soldiers guard a beer cart loaded with barrels and a tax wagon as they wind through what has now become a dangerous Sherwood Forest. The wagon is an armoured box on wheels, with crossbow slits at the side. Guy of Gisborne, right hand man to the Sheriff of Nottingham, commands the escort.

Gisborne anxiously eyes the shadows of the forest. Most of the men are on edge. But the beer cart is steered by a fat red-faced Friar, raucously singing hymns and quaffing from a jug which he repeatedly dips into one of the barrels.

As Gisborne turns to him once more to urge silence, arrows start to whistle in from nowhere. The Friar yells and drops his jug as a soldier is hit. At the forest edge four woodsmen come in to view; they fire again and run down a narrow path. The mounted guard give chase, slashing at the thick brush.

Robin and Azeem swing from the trees onto the tax wagon, kicking the two drivers to the ground. They take the reins and steer it off the road. The archers inside are unable to fire at them.

Little John leaps on to the beer cart, sending the Friar crashing back among the barrels. The Friar slams his head hard and drops unconscious. John whips the horse, driving the cart after Robin. A camouflage screen is lifted into place, covering their route in the forest. Gisborne and his men race back to the road. The wagons are gone. Gisborne rides frantically back and forth, searching and cursing.

Deeper in the forest, Robin tells the soldiers inside the wagon: "Surrender your weapons. I give you my word you shall go free." In reply, a swordblade is jabbed through the roof from below.

He and Azeem steer the tax wagon into the river and jump clear. Water floods through the slits. Like rats, the soldiers soon abandon ship. Later, Little John swings an axe to open up the strong box. Robin and his men react with astonishment as they gaze into a treasure chest, filled to the brim with glittering gold coins.

The Friar has come round at last and is fighting with some of Robin's men. "Get off him," orders Robin. "He is a man of the

A coach (LEFT) filled with bullion is diverted by the outlaws, who attack the armed guard (BELOW). Wulf attaches grappling hooks to the wagon to disable it (RIGHT).

cloth." The Friar clambers to his feet. Around him are battered and winded woodsmen.

"The Lord's blessing on you, kind sir," he says. "These sinners were attempting to steal the libations destined for the monks of St. Catherine's." The Friar climbs back onto his wagon.

"A moment, my reverend friend," says Robin, as he grabs the horse's bridle. "You travel with poor company when you travel with Nottingham's soldiers."

To cheers and shouts from his men, Robin adds: "I am Robin of Locksley and my men are thirsty."

The Friar mockingly crosses himself for their benefit: "Lord bless me, sir," he says. "I had mistook you and your men for common thieves. So if you wish them to share in the good Lord's brew...".

He reaches under the seat, pulls out a club and smites Robin with it. As Robin staggers, the Friar whips up his horse. But, obese as his driver, the horse slowly raises his head from the grass and ambles forward as the Friar turns and yells: "Confess Robin Hood that Friar Tuck is a better, holier and braver man than thou art!"

A low hanging branch hits Tuck on the back of the head, tumbling him from the cart. Robin and his men then take him, the captive soldiers, the gold bullion and the beer back to their camp. It has been a most successful day.

Tuck surveys the crowd of hopeful, hungry faces and the little hamlet of half-built huts. "Well Friar Tuck," says Robin, "are these not here the meek of the Earth? We have need of an honest man of God to minister to them. What say you, Friar?" Tuck folds his hands in a moment of prayer. "The Lord moves in mysterious ways," he says. "I accept." "You won't regret it," says Robin. "Aye, but you may," grins Tuck.

Friar Tuck, who had been travelling with the Sheriff's protection, is restrained by Bull (ABOVE), but receives Robin's blessing (LEFT) and joins the outlaws.

Battle at the Tree House Camp

As dawn breaks in Robin's forest encampment, the overnight look-out spots a rider some distance away. He fires a warning arrow in to the camp. The warning brings Robin and other stirring woodsmen running to that side of their camp. They look up to the sentry, who is silently pointing towards the approaching horse and rider. Robin is relieved as he recognizes the rider as Duncan, his father's old and now-blind retainer. He runs out to meet the old man, who collapses in his arms.

"Duncan - what happened?"

"I found you, Master Robin. Thank God I did it...Nottingham's men attacked us."

" Marian?"

"They took her."

But more warning arrows come from the look-outs. Azeem raises his telescope, scanning the forest. Two hundred yards away, the hilltop is lined with horsemen. Celt mercenaries, hired by the Sheriff to discover and destroy Robin and his men, gaze down. Clad in hides and skins, with painted arms and faces, they stand in eerie silence.

Observes Will Scarlett: "The stupid old man has led them right to us!"

Behind the Celtic Chieftain is the Sheriff, dressed in full armour: "I want prisoners," he tells him.

There follows the most bitter and bloody battle between the unwarlike woodsmen and the armoured soldiers and mercenaries.

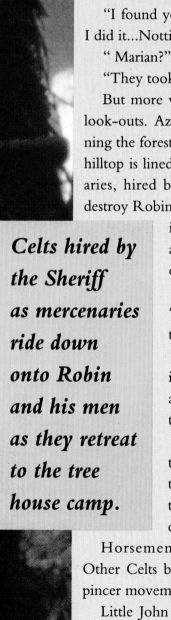

Celts hired by the Sheriff as mercenaries ride down onto Robin and his men as they retreat to the tree house camp.

Horsemen charge through the trees. Other Celts break to the left and right in a pincer movement.

Little John screams at his men, who run

to various battle stations. Women and children clamber up into the trees. Robin, stranded near Duncan, fires four arrows in rapid succession, killing the leading horsemen. Azeem swings his scimitar. Duncan, overwhelmed with guilt for bringing the enemy to the camp, grapples blindly for a sword from a fallen Celt and charges into the oncoming hordes.

Robin runs back to the camp and urges his men to climb ladders to the fortified treehouse network. The woodsmen cut down the ladders behind them with axes; Celts, already clambering after them, fall to their deaths 40 feet below.

Robin's men seem to be on top of the battle as they exchange arrow-volleys. But a ball of fire shudders through the treetops from a catapult missile and the Celts deliver a stream of flaming arrows. The camp is set alight. Tuck and the woodsmen yank on their water pulleys, distributing water buckets in human chains. But the fire has become too intense.

The men pull out emergency ropes and ladders from the tree houses and scramble down with the women and children. The village is abandoned, with Little John, Azeem and a handful of the men in full retreat. Then Robin tumbles to the ground amid the flaming debris and carnage.

The battle rages round the camp with the outlaws fighting back bravely. But a ball of fire shudders through the treetops.

The Hanging of the Woodsmen

The Sheriff of Nottingham decides on a public hanging in the city square for ten of the captured woodsmen, including young Wulf, son of Little John and Fanny, as an example to others. Other woodsmen and their families will go free – so long as Maid Marian agrees to marry the Sheriff. Faced with such an offer, she reluctantly nods her agreement.

The Sheriff orders that the ten victims be tortured first as the gallows are built in the square. In a surprising twist, Will Scarlett offers to check if Robin has died in the fire – and kill him if he still lives in exchange for a return to his own life. The Sheriff agrees.

Meanwhile, Robin, who has survived the camp attack, is reunited in the forest with Little John, Azeem and Friar Tuck. Robin feels like he has failed his friends. Along with Bull and Fanny they bury the burned bodies of many of their men. Will finds them and fully

BELOW: Will awaits the executioner's axe.

informs Robin of the deal he has made with the Sheriff. He also brings news of the intended hanging and the planned marriage. Will demands of the despondent Robin that they continue to fight. Will's words stir Robin's courage. All the survivors pledge to fight to the end. Robin then plans how they they can help their men escape.

On the day of the hanging, soldiers prod and harass the peasants who stream to the city square. They pass a pile of confiscated weapons – daggers and the like.

Accompanied by a beggar, swaddled from head to toe in bandages, Friar Tuck drives a cartload of barrels past the soldiers. Fanny is behind them carrying a huge woven basket.

Bull arrives, disguised as a Celt; Little John climbs the castle wall, aided by Fanny; a pile of firewood sticks is hauled up with him. Dozens of arrows and a few swords are camouflaged within.

But the plans seem to go wrong when Wulf, being led to the gallows, recognizes Will Scarlett through his disguise. He rushes at him, fists flailing, accusing him of being a traitor to the outlaw's cause. Soldiers grab Wulf and throw him to the ground. The Sheriff sees the uproar from his vantage point and orders that Will be hauled before him. "Ah, the turncoat," he says, recogniz-

FT: Little John climbs the
ottingham Castle walls,
ith Fanny waiting for
m, while Friar Tuck
des in on a wagon with
bin in disguise. RIGHT
ND BELOW: The hanging
egins and Wulf goes
rst. Little John rushes the
bbet, covered by an
plosion in the square.

> **"...or do we band together as brothers should and save those who would save us?"**

The wagon and barrels - which are packed with explosives - go up in an enormous sheet of flame. The executioner starts moving down the line of condemned men, kicking away the stools. But Tuck cudgels his way to the gibbet, crying "Make way, sinners." Nine men

ing him. The Sheriff orders that Will be executed with the other woodsmen.

In the hanging, Wulf is first. The sight of the executioner kicking the stool from under their son's feet drives Fanny and Little John into wild action. Robin discards his beggar's disguise and raises his hidden bow to fire at the noose. As Wulf's face is turning blue an arrow partly severs the rope; Robin fires another which slices the rope completely.

Azeem looses a fire-tipped arrow at Tuck's wagon, which has been left by the city wall.

dance on their ropes as Tuck and the released Wulf try to save them. Bull attacks the executioner. Little John, roaring angrily, also reaches the scaffold, slamming his huge body into the timber. The upright collapses under such constant, frantic battering, taking the gibbet with it. All pressure is released from the men's necks. Little John, Bull and Tuck start cutting the ropes to save their friends.

The Taking of Nottingham Castle

Onlookers, inspired at what they have seen, turn as one on the outnumbered soldiers. Revolution is in the air as fallen weapons are grabbed. They clamber to get at the barons, who have joined the Sheriff on the balcony overlooking the scene. Armed with a sword, Robin dodges missiles fired by the soldiers and sees Marian being dragged under an arch into the heart of the castle.

The Sheriff marches through with Marian: "Seal the entrance," he orders. "Guard it with your lives. Bring the Bishop to my chapel."

The Sheriff orders the Bishop to marry him and Marian immediately. Robin and Azeem race down castle corridors, searching for the pair. Soldiers and armed servants converge to block their way. But the two of them strike and kick their way deeper into the castle. Robin grabs a soldier and forces him to reveal the whereabouts of Marian and the Sheriff.

The Bishop is nervously stumbling through the Latin portion of the marriage ceremony as Robin and Azeem use a stone statue of the Sheriff to try and batter down the chapel door. But the door holds fast. Robin looking for another way in finds some steps which lead up onto the roof. He rips down a long pennant fluttering in the breeze, secures it tightly to the battlements and swings over the wall.

He aims his feet at a stained glass window below as the Sheriff grapples Marian to the stone floor, ripping at her dress as he does so. Robin crashes through the glass behind the altar and rolls to his feet. The Bishop flees. Robin pulls his sword and announces to the Sheriff: "Here is your divorce."

ABOVE: *While Azeem is trying to break into the chapel, Mortianna appears and attacks him. He manages to turn her own spear into her.* **LEFT:** *Marian is forced to marry the Sheriff.* **RIGHT:** *Robin breaks into the chapel to save Marian; a fierce sword fight ensues. Just as the Sheriff is about to execute the coup de grace, Robin stabs him to the heart with Marian's dagger.*

torn to shreds: tapestries are sliced down, pews are hacked to bits and the swords knock chunks of stone from columns and walls.

In the Sheriff's hand Robin's father's sword has by far the better blade and eventually breaks his own. As the Sheriff moves in for the kill, Robin desperately pulls a dagger from his jacket which Marian had given him and thrusts it deep into the Sheriff's heart.

The Sheriff in turn quickly unsheathes his sword. "I killed your father with this - his own sword," baits the Sheriff. "Appropriate, don't you think, that I now use it to send you to meet him."

A furious fight follows. The Chapel is

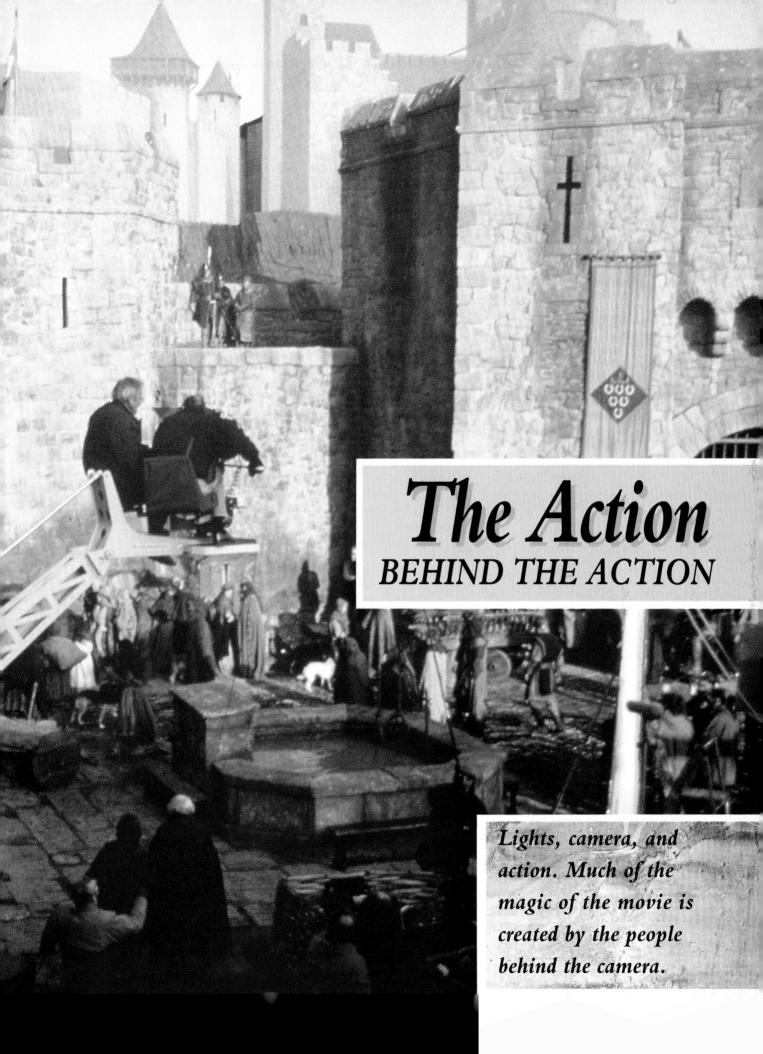

The Action
BEHIND THE ACTION

Lights, camera, and action. Much of the magic of the movie is created by the people behind the camera.

The Director

"For some reason, certain subjects capture the public's imagination – and this is one of them. I try not to think about it, to be honest. I have never been one for hype."

While the script and film action concentrates on the enemies of the people and Robin Hood, there was only one enemy in sight for director KEVIN REYNOLDS: time.

From his first involvement to the point of the film being ready for screening is less than a year. Fast, he kept on saying. Far too fast. Reynolds was given a deadline and told to deliver a top-quality product: "I knew what I was in for right from the start," he admits. "The prospect of cutting corners or accepting second-best to meet the deadline was rejected by us all. We have gone for the very best possible.

"But I came into this picture only ten weeks before we started shooting. We have been struggling from day one as a result. The problem has never left us. We started in September with the English autumn already upon us. With each day there was a prospect of worsening weather and less light. By the time we got closer to Christmas, we were down to six hours of usable light a day."

Reynolds started his dark dawns at 5 a.m. He was never finished before midnight after watching the results of the day's filming and preparing for the following 24 hours.

But despite the pressures and lack of sleep, he had an unusual calmness which had a positive effect on every person on set. "Generally, I am fairly calm by nature," he said. "I find that if people scream and shout a lot on set then after a while no-one pays them any attention. It is a waste of energy. I think it is more important to try and inspire people rather than crush them. Take that approach and most people do respond to it."

The fact that Reynolds had already signed

to the film did sway the eventual decision of Kevin Costner to become *this* Robin Hood, as opposed to the other offers he received. The two have been friends for nine years. Yet when they first met, Reynolds was making a small-budget film school picture which needed an actor to play a comic role: "I gave the part to someone else," he now reveals.

"I thought this other guy had a better comic timing. The other guy is still doing bit-parts around Los Angeles and Kevin is one of the world's biggest stars. I wish I could now say: 'Yes, I saw a big future for Kevin.' But I can't. He certainly had some sort of charisma then and seemed to know what he wanted. Yet, beyond that...? I suppose most of all he had no self-doubts, stuck to what he wanted to do and had the talent to back his faith and judgement."

Also, that first meeting made sufficient impact on Reynolds to make him want to cast Kevin Costner in his debut movie, *Fandango* in 1984. The director is now in a unique position to assess the special qualities in Kevin Costner which fill cinemas across the world.

"He's got charisma with a capital C," he says. "The camera loves him from any angle. He really seems to have his finger on the pulse of what the public want to see - his instincts are so good and he follows them. He also has a certain natural presence. That is a quality which has developed with success. One success leads to another and that in turn develops into total confidence.

"As a friend, he is very open. Definitely one of the guys. We are interested in the same sort of things and have a basic, middle America background. His feet are firmly on the ground at all times.

"I know it has been very difficult for him to keep his head on straight - to hold on to a

sense of reality - with all that has gone on in the last few years. But he does it."

Reynolds cannot explain why Robin Hood has suddenly become the hottest legendary character in Hollywood: "For some reason, certain subjects capture the public's imagination - and this is one of them," he says. "I try not to think about it, to be honest. I have never been one for hype."

But he was crystal clear on what he

"As a friend, he is very open. Definitely one of the guys. His feet are firmly on the ground at all times," says Kevin Reynolds of his star.

wanted from the movie: "I wanted to make it look realistic," he says. "I can relate to something much more strongly if it feels real. That gives us the chance to cross the line of making something realistic - and take that occassional fantastic step. I am also trying to expand the boundaries of each character, because I hate one dimensional action movies."

And have things gone perfectly to plan? "You always start a picture with something that is perfect in your mind and it's compromise from there," he says. "I don't know anyone yet who ever thought a picture went perfectly. But, yes, *Prince of Thieves* is as perfect as it can be at this moment."

Morgan Creek
PRODUCTIONS

JAMES G. ROBINSON is the founder and owner of Morgan Creek Productions, one of the most successful independent production companies in Hollywood. GARY BARBER and DAVID NICKSAY are Chief Operating Officer and President of Morgan Creek Productions respectively. All three were critically involved in the 10-hour decision to acquire the Prince of Thieves script:

"I heard through the grapevine that there was a very hot screenplay on Robin Hood, so I arranged to receive the script on February 13th, 1990," stated Nicksay.

"I took it home that evening and asked two members of our staff to also take it home. We all read it overnight, discussed it the next morning and, by noon of February 14th - Saint Valentine's Day - were determined to get it.

"We all thought that this was commercial, distinctive and great fun, and that Morgan Creek could really make it work. I walked over to Gary's [Barber] office and said there's this great screenplay by John Watson and Pen Densham and, since you know them, why don't you give them a call?" Said Gary Barber, "David then gave me a 'pitch' on the movie, and I called John and Pen and said we love your script and would really like to do the movie.

"John and Pen were really excited and said I should call Mike Simpson [their agent at William Morris]. I called Mike and made a very aggressive offer, contingent upon Jim's [Robinson] 'concurrence'. After all, it was a multi-million dollar decision, but David and I suspected Jim would agree."

Nicksay said, "We found there was interest from other sources, too. It was late afternoon and we needed to confer with Jim Robinson, who was flying into Los Angeles from our corporate headquarters in Baltimore, Maryland."

"As soon as I got into the car - the phone rang," continued Robinson. "I asked Gary and David, 'Can't this wait until tomorrow?' They both said no! They were exuberant about the script, so I thought that if they were this enthusiastic and both agree on the screenplay (which isn't often), then it must

LEFT TO RIGHT: James G. Robinson, Gary Barber and David Nicksay, the executive producers at Morgan Creek.

be special. I went straight to the office, delayed my planned dinner, and we began reviewing the project."

"We called Mike Simpson and said that we were removing the contingency, but advised that the offer would expire in three hours, at 10 pm."

Said Barber, "At 9:50 that evening, we concluded the deal with Mike Simpson." Adds Robinson: "As a company, it is our policy to act both quickly and decisively. This definitely gives us a competitive edge over our rivals. We are designed to move fast, with calculated precision. If we lose that edge, it just puts us back in the pack with everyone else."

Barber commented: "I think that John and Pen knew that, when Morgan Creek bought the screenplay, the movie was going to be made. Hollywood is full of people who have bought movie scripts with great fanfare and enthusiasm - and then the project ends up on the shelf."

James G. Robinson is obviously delighted to have Kevin Costner in the lead role: "It was not vital to get a huge star, but to get a megastar like Kevin is great. We had the three top star actors in mind, but never had to go past Number One on the list. Kevin's name first came into the frame on February 19th - so you can imagine how pleased we were to eventually get him.

"When we talked to Kevin, he said, 'I am a running and jumping actor. Horses, swooping out of trees, bows and arrows, sword fighting. It [the script] has so much for me.'"

There was never any doubt that the film would be made in England: "We felt we would get much better results," says Nicksay. "The technical knowledge of the film people here is superb."

Adds Robinson: "We thought we would get a more accurate observation by making this production with a British crew on British soil. After all, Robin Hood is the very essence of England."

Trilogy
ENTERTAINMENT GROUP

The *Robin Hood: Prince of Thieves* producer team of JOHN WATSON, PEN DENSHAM, who are both English, and their American partner RICHARD LEWIS work in Hollywood under the company banner, the Trilogy Entertainment Group. They consider their company's logo, a circle within a triangle, a graphic expression of their filmmaking philosophy. A sharing and combining of the three's individual strengths and talents to make an effective creative force.

"We like to think of ourselves as a kind of motion picture Three Musketeers," says Densham, "One for all, and all for one."

Watson, Densham and Lewis have distinguished themselves as award-winning writer-director-producers. "We start from the strongest foundation, our scripts" says Richard Lewis. "We regard ourselves as a filmmaking think-tank, and encourage creative debate amongst ourselves and those we work with."

Robin Hood was created from just such an internal dialogue. Densham created the basic story and then collaborated with Watson writing the screenplay. "We're both English, so we used Richard as a kind of 'guinea pig,' just to make sure that the script made sense to an American audience too."

Once the script was completed Lewis teamed with Mike Simpson to create what was perhaps the most intense selling frenzy to hit Hollywood in 1990. Lewis culminated the negotiating marathon on February 14th. "We were under immense pressure to make a decision very quickly, it required a cool head. Despite offers that on the surface appeared more remunerative, we elected to place our script with Morgan Creek because they shared our vision and I believed they really had the commitment to get *Robin Hood: Prince of Thieves* made."

John Watson
PRODUCER AND CO-SCRIPTWRITER

JOHN WATSON, who with fellow Englishman Pen Densham, wrote the script of *Robin Hood: Prince of Thieves*, has at last realized an ambition of the last five years - to deliver the sort of script on English folklore that Hollywood would take to its heart.

"After talking about it for so long, we did did not really get the writing together on this until the start of 1989," says John. "Pen Densham suddenly hit on the idea of Robin being captured while on the Crusades. We should start with him in jail, escaping.

"During the escape two things happen to shape the story. His best friend is killed. He turns out to be the brother of Marian and his dying wish is that Robin should look after his sister. He also escapes with another prisoner - a Moor - and saves his life. The Moor believes that he should stay with Robin until he has a chance to save *his* life too.

"We felt this was a fresh and exciting way of reintroducing the Robin Hood story. Also, what does coming home mean for Robin? Things have changed.

"Robin has had his nobility taken away and the Sheriff of Nottingham wants to return to the Dark Ages and the black arts that were prevalent in England during that time. So it is Robin versus evil. Robin's

father has been falsely accused and killed. He has to avenge him, too. All of this sets the scene and we introduce the traditional characters to join him, like Little John and Friar Tuck."

On the dialogue, John says: "It is a tough call, because we wanted dialogue to 'feel' right. It has a flavour of earlier times - as you can believe people spoke in those times - but it has to be for a modern audience."

And how about the mixture of accents? "We have an interesting blend of British and American voices, which I think will be accepted when people hear them. We have asked dialogue coaches to soften American accents, without making them sound English. I think it's something that will only be noticed (if at all) in the United Kingdom.

"Getting the film into production was a wild ride," John recounts. "Not only were we in a race with two other planned Robin Hood pictures but we knew we had to start filming in September so that we could guarantee having leaves on our Sherwood Forest trees. I ended up in the extraordinary situation of hiring the Production Designer and ten other Heads of Department before we had decided on our Director. Fortunately, Kevin Reynolds loved my choices and we were able to start on time."

Pen Densham
STORY CREATOR AND PRODUCER

PEN DENSHAM fought a long, hard battle to get Robin Hood on screen before even an arrow was drawn in anger. Yet the English-born Producer was determined that it was a battle to be won.

The reason was his own conviction that Robin's story could not only be a great adventure, but also an emotionally uplifting

LEFT TO RIGHT: Pen Densham, John Watson and Richard Lewis.

movie which would win followers throughout the world. "I wanted to put a Christian and Moor side by side to face evil together," he says. "Also, Robin going off to the Crusades was something that so many families could identify with. It is like a son going to Vietnam, saying to his father ★★★★ you, and then returning to find his whole world had changed. I saw Robin as a man filled with complex emotions.

"How could he be motivated? He returns to find himself and the peasants having something in common: their will to stand up against dark forces and fight. I am a Pacifist, but I realize there are moments in life when there is nothing to do but fight for what you believe is right."

Densham, born in London to a cameraman father Ray Densham - Pen's full name is Penray - left school at 15 and moved to Canada to make films at the age of 19.

He is now 40 and finally getting credited for "overnight success" with Trilogy and partners, fellow Brit John Watson and Richard Lewis, in the face of a strong 20-year track record.

He toiled long and hard over his computer screen at Trilogy offices based in futuristic-looking Century City, Los Angeles, re-creating a story from 12th Century England.

"The ideas would start flowing in the shower each morning and still be ticking over when I went to bed at midnight," he reports. "I even kept a pencil and pad at the bedside for when I woke up in the middle of the night."

In spite of such efforts three major film companies he met to discuss his ideas told him: "Forget it. Costume epics don't sell." He persisted and against all professional advice continued to write. Once the script was complete then the offers began to flow.

Suddenly, detractors could see potential: "I am very proud of our achievements at Trilogy in getting this on screen," says Pen Densham "It is the culmination of six years work and non-stop effort."

Production Designer

ABOVE: *Nottingham Castle and Square as designed by John Graysmark's production team and constructed on the back lot at Shepperton Studios just outside London.*

When production designer JOHN GRAYSMARK was told that he could have a free hand in making the film look realistically 12th Century he breathed a sigh of relief. He has long hated the "clean" appearance of so many historical movies: "The truth is that it was a filthy time of dark days, freezing castles, colourless clothes, limited food and no hygiene," he says. "We have tried to get as close to what we now research as 'the truth', without making the film a history lesson."

After getting the all-clear from director Kevin Reynolds and Morgan Creek,

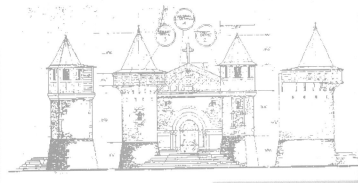

John's first task was to draw up plans of everything in the film - from Robin Hood's camp in Sherwood Forest to the smallest dagger.

ABOVE AND LEFT: **Two of the 600 detailed drawings produced by the art department.**

He and his art department of ten master-minded 600 separate drawings, as a precise guide for set-builders and craftsmen who made the swords and shields.

Graysmark, whose first of two Oscar nominations came in 1972 with *Young Winston*, is a stickler for detail: he would not even let a sheep or goat be used which did not comply with what would have been seen in the 1190s.

"In those days, a full-grown cow was the size of a Great Dane," he reports.

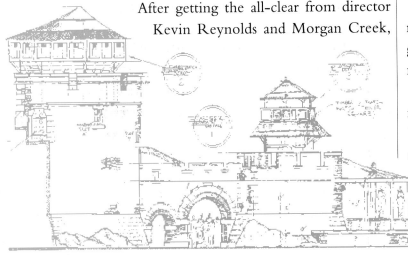

BELOW: *The fantastic tree camp in Sherwood Forest as it was visualized by the production design team, and the finished set, built on location by craftsmen and by the film's technicians.*

"And pigs were round, pink little things. We have bred them bigger and bigger over the years to get more bacon. Then there were the sheep: very shaggy things in those days. It's the same with birds. We have integrated many breeds of geese over the centuries, for example, and what we shoot and eat now are very different in shape and size. Fortunately, there are breeds that you can still get which have been undiluted by time and breeding. Although it took time and the animals are only seen in background shots, we thought it worth it.

they did not realize it at the time, the boiling of the water killed all the germs. It would have been a weak alcohol in those days, drunk from cups made of leather or wood."

Graysmark rigorously researched each scene: "The city square in Nottingham gave us the most problems," he reports. "The Romans would have first settled the city. So we had to try and amalgamate their style with those of the Vikings and Saxons, with the major Norman buildings added.

"In truth, of course, there would have been some brand *new* buildings around that time. But since audiences would not accept that, we had to make them look old by sandblasting, to get the grain out of the wood.

"We have tried to get as close to what we now research as 'the truth', without making the film a history lesson."

JOHN GRAYSMARK, PRODUCTION DESIGNER

"In one scene we have an original walled garden. Again, it was very important to only have vegetables on display that would have been grown in the 12th Century. The staple diet then was turnips, swede and bread. Drink everywhere was beer or mead. Mead was honey, which was watered down and allowed to ferment.

"Every castle, priory or home of any stature had its own beer. The water was so dreadful the only way they could get a decent taste was to make beer. Although

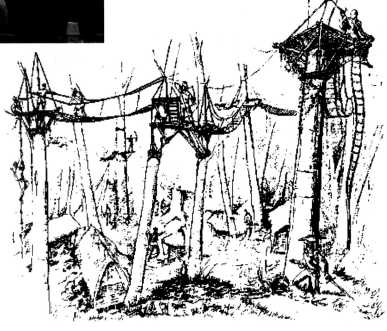

Production Designer

"In the city square, all trades would have been there with their stalls. Often, they were the most unlikely ones: a thong-maker, for example, who would have been very busy since thongs were used so widely for ties of all sorts. But there were no butchers or bakers. There were millers, who would mill grain for you at their mill houses and you would take it home to make bread. And a butcher would kill a cow to share around several families for immediate use but there was no way of storing meat beyond that."

So John Graysmark set about pulling apart the myths of Robin Hood - while endeavouring to keep the romance of the legend.

On colours, he says: "There would not have been a green tunic in sight. All the woodsmen would have been dressed in cloth of earth colours. In fact, green and blue were the two most difficult - and exclusive - pigments. Green was sometimes used for the painting of castle interiors. Blue was expensive - because it was from lapis, ground down - and used only by the Church because it was rich enough to pay the price. We use blue for the inside of the Bishop's room in the film."

But although the true colours of Nottingham Castle would have been red and white, John believes that is stretching authenticity too far.

"Audiences would have the greatest difficulty in believing it," he says. "The exterior of Nottingham Castle, which we always imagined was a splendid stone colour, was actually painted white and the joints were painted red. The idea was that when you came through the forest there was this great white thing in front of you, looming up from nowhere. It struck terror into the peasants. It also killed off all bugs and lice in the castle walls. They used lime and painted as high as possible. Or they would pour it over the walls from the battlements."

The bows and arrows are based on accurate sizes: "They were around 5 feet 6 inches long, mostly used for hunting in the forest. They would be made of yew, with arrows from a straight-grained wood like beech. A village blacksmith made the heads and children gathered goose feathers to make the flights. They would make good weapons, but are not to be confused with the longbow which came around 100 years later. The longbow, 6 feet with a massive yew grip of around two inches diameter, had an effective range of 350 yards and could pierce armour

ABOVE LEFT: *John Graysmark, Production Designer extraordinaire, on the set he designed.* **LEFT:** *The background of the castle is revealed.*

plate at that distance. The bows we are using would have an accurate, effective range of about half that."

There are many superb sets, but two of them need particular mention. Nottingham Castle Square was built at Shepperton Studios, Surrey on the back lot; and Robin's camp was constructed in the heart of woodland at Burnham Beeches, Buckinghamshire, which had a public right of way only 50 yards from the set.

Far from neatly-dressed, smiling "merry men" - a phrase not mentioned in the entire film - the woodsmen would have had a rather wet, cold and grim time living deep in the forest. "The homes, if you can call them that, were constructed from woven willow twigs,

patched over with mud and straw, with cow dung and cow hair," says John. "We used plaster on location, but tried to get that sort of effect. On the roofs we used sapling poles with thin twigs. A thatching company did the work for us."

So given John's long experience in production design and love of historical research, were there any surprises, or errors of authenticity?

"There could have easily been a simple slip-up with the blacksmith's anvil. We discovered that the anvil used for weapon-making would be curved at both ends, for left and right-handed weapons, shaped like a pair of bull's horns. But that is the thing about this business. We're learning all the time."

ABOVE AND LEFT: *John Graysmark's original design for the hamlet near Nottingham and how it eventually looked when it was constructed.*

ABOVE AND LEFT: *The design sketch and the finished, dressed set, a corridor in Nottingham Castle. The Sheriff's living quarter's are through the archway on the left.*

Costume Designer

JOHN BLOOMFIELD'S biggest problem was to make new costumes look as if they had been worn in the forest, night and day, for years.

First, he ordered several thousand yards of basic fabric in white. Then he and a team of 50 costume-makers set to work on 1,000 separate outfits, using a dye of vegetable colours in a variety of browns. Next, they used 150 cheese-graters and wire brushes on the clothes to age them until they looked almost completely worn-out.

John's brief was to go for authenticity in virtually everything. He only departed completely from history in the making of Maid Marian's wedding dress.

"I used all silk," he says. "It is wrong for the period, but we are not doing something for a museum. I had silk organza boiling for ten hours. It ended up looking like really fine muslin, which you just can't buy. And it took two people two weeks to make it."

Other particularly striking outfits are Robin's wedding suit and the clothes for King Richard. "I had to make King Richard's before we knew who had accepted the part," says John. "But I guessed whoever they chose would be around 6 feet 1 inch tall with a 44 inch chest. It was absolutely ideal."

Each of the main characters have several outfits. Costner's Robin Hood has five: as a prisoner; a pilgrim, returning to England; a woodsman; a disguise as a soldier to enter Nottingham castle; and his wedding suit.

Marian has seven. Her first costume is a man's (she is wearing a mask to disguise her); her "at home" dress; riding outfit; another dress for going to church; dressing gown for a night scene; and two wedding dresses, the first of which came as a gift from the Sheriff,

FAR LEFT: *John Bloomfield, the costume designer, in his studio. Robin's marriage costume sketch stands next to him, in front of Lord Locksley's costume.* LEFT: *The Sheriff and Azeem's costumes.* BELOW LEFT AND BOTTOM: *The sketch for King Richard's costume and for Marian's wedding dress.* RIGHT: *Peter Young, set decorator.*

who is desperate to marry her.

The Sheriff has six costumes: a swirling robe, the first time we see him; armour; priest's outfit, for his religious sect; a black outfit, with studs, which he wears in the castle; a robe for attending a Cathedral; and his suit for the wedding attempt with Marian.

"But each costume for every main character has to be duplicated three or four times," reveals Bloomfield. "They have to be available for 'doubles' - in other words, back shots only - and stunt men. Also, there must be a spare outfit ready in case of unforeseen circumstances, like a tear or damage."

Little John (Nick Brimble) had the most of any one costume: *six* of his basic outfit. "Several of them were used in his fight in the water with Robin," says John. And has anyone asked to keep their costume? Only one: Kevin Costner kept his wedding suit.

Set Decorator

PETER YOUNG, an Academy-Award winning set decorator, is in no doubt about his biggest problem on Robin Hood: "It is matching the arrows to each scene," he says.

"The real arrow is supposed to be made of a birch shaft with white goose quill and a steel barbed tip. What we have, in fact, are arrows made completely of rubber for firing into crowds, arrows of fibreglass which pop up in the ground for special effects - plus the real things. The trouble is, they all *look* the same to the eye."

That, of course, is the mark of a team of 23 successful props craftsmen. And Peter, whose job as set decorator is to provide props to fit in with John Graysmark's general look of the film, is in charge of them all. "It started with a buyer and myself going through all the details of things from swords, arrows and axes to tapestries," he says.

There were 100 of Robin's men, each supplied with a bow, quiver, a set of 10 arrows, and staves and cudgels. The idea was to give them a basic, rustic look. Then came the 150 Celts. They had axes, spears, crossbows, round shields and daggers. The 200 Sheriff's men, who Young always refers to as "Nottingham's men", were supplied with at least one of the following: an axe, sword, crossbow and dagger.

"Weapons are made of fibreglass, rubber, dural (a light steel) and steel itself," says Young. "Hopefully, I can tell with the naked eye which is which - apart from the arrows."

The range of different models for just one weapon, though, caused more problems.

This amazing catapult used by the Sheriff's men to destroy the woodsmen's camp, was constructed from original 13th Century designs.

LEFT: Some of the many weapons that Peter Young provided. The Celts had swords, axes, shields and clubs.
ABOVE: Robin takes aim - the attention to detail is evident in the goose feathers used on the arrows.
BELOW: The Sheriff uses his weapon.

There were *ten* versions of the sword taken from Robin's father by the Sheriff of Nottingham:

1. Lightweight, made of rubber.

2. Lightweight, of fibre glass.

3. Retractable, made of fibre glass, which can cause sparks to fly when struck on stone walls.

4. Retractable, when plunged into the body.

5. Retractable, used sideways.

6. Real one, made of steel.

7. Real one, lightweight steel, for fencing only.

8. Another real one, of lightweight steel, for fencing only - as a back-up.

9. One larger than usual, so it will look cumbersome in the Sheriff's hands when he tries to use it.

10. One smaller than usual, so that when Robin picks it up he can use one hand only and swing it around expertly.

Peter, whose past films have included *Batman* (1990), all the *Superman* films and *Supergirl* (1984), is used to creating such illusions. "But when they fool me, I know they are really good," he says.

Stunt Co-ordinator

Kevin Costner caused stunt co-ordinator PAUL WESTON some heart-stopping moments. Paul, internationally known for his work on the James Bond movies, constantly urged Costner to play it safe.

"I had to stop him doing quite a few things that would have put him at risk," says Paul. "Even so, he still pushed everything to its boundaries. I would be watching as he would lean out a little too far to give the best possible shot for the director. He would be hanging out of a tree, for example, with a 30-foot drop below, and my heart would be in my mouth.

"Although he is an actor who enjoys the action, I had to tell him:'It's not worth putting yourself into a situation where you can be badly injured. It's not good for you, not good for the film and it's not safe for others around you.'"

Costner was insistent on doing one particular action sequence, in which Robin swings from tree to tree: "He wanted to do them free-hand," said Weston. "That is fine for one take, but by the seventh the director might still not be satisfied. So what happens then? I do not want to put any actor into a situation where there is a considerable risk of danger.

"So he went into a harness right from the start. You can never tell with these things. With each take, a little more strength and timing and concentration can disappear."

Paul, with 25 years in the business and a reputation for always going where the film action is at its most frantic - he masterminded *Aliens* (1986) and both *Superman II* (1980) and *Superman III* (1983) - is a thoughtful, intelligent operator who always protects the actors. Despite tremendous strength and agility, he is a quietly-spoken man who believes in thinking through every sequence.

"Every time I do any job I go to the top and take it through in my own mind - the thought process of exactly what is going to happen through stand-by, turn-over and

Behind the Action

Two well co-ordinated stunt sequences organized by Paul Weston. LEFT: A woodsman knocks a soldier off his horse by swinging on a rope from one of the trees. RIGHT: A Celt tries to climb into the tree camp but his rope is cut and he falls to the ground. BELOW LEFT: Paul Weston on the set with the director Kevin Reynolds.

action," he explains. "How am I going to fall? How am I going to hit the rig? Are there going to be any noises? Am I going to be shot at? Do I turn in the air?

"Then, when the director wants another take I will go through the same process again. So if someone says: 'We are losing the light - let's go for this action quickly,' I can have what I am doing very clearly in my mind. It is complacency that leads to sloppiness which in turn leads to injury."

Paul was responsible for hand-picking the 80 stunt men in *Robin Hood: Prince of Thieves* and briefing them carefully in his policy of working. Obviously, many have worked with him before. But he still takes them through a refresher course on his views and beliefs each time.

"I have used some new guys on this and it gives me a chance to watch their attitudes," he says. "I like good workers. I don't want people sitting around, getting bored or not taking notice. We know that it can be a bit off-putting to be on a film set hour after hour just waiting to be called into action, but you must never let your guard drop.

"As a stunt co-ordinator I do not let a producer or director push me in to a corner.

Safety is the most important thing. The safety of the artist and of the stunt man."

Even so, the equipment itself can not always be guaranteed. When Paul was working on *Superman II*, one of the wires broke. He fell on his head, broke his cheekbone and suffered a badly gashed hand.

And on *Return of the Jedi* (1983), another stunt man's wires broke. He fell directly on to Paul, breaking his leg. Thankfully, there were no such unforeseen accidents on *Robin Hood*. "We get knocks and bruises all the time, but we grit our teeth and get on with it. That's why they pay us."

He had particular admiration for Costner's dedication and the incredible fitness of Morgan Freeman: "Morgan is probably the fittest actor on this set," he says. "He works out each day and is like a powerhouse. He used to be a

Behind the Action

Various action sequences were first worked out with storyboards. These gave everyone concerned a better idea on how to plan the stunts, lighting, camera angles, etc.

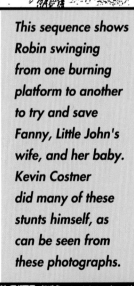

This sequence shows Robin swinging from one burning platform to another to try and save Fanny, Little John's wife, and her baby. Kevin Costner did many of these stunts himself, as can be seen from these photographs.

Stunt Double

SIMON CRANE is 6 feet tall, weighs 168 lbs, has a chest of 40 inches, a waist of 31 inches and wears a 7-inch hat. With those vital statistics, Simon acted as the stunt double for Kevin Costner in the same fearless style as he did with James Bond actor Timothy Dalton

> **"He grabs hold of a banner, jumps from the castle wall and swings down through a window using the banner as a rope. It was a tough one to do."**

dancer and has perfect co-ordination. When he is not working out in the gymnasium at Shepperton Studios, he's back at the gym in his London hotel."

But Paul, as ever, gives a direct view on their efforts: "Stunt men would honestly like the actors to act - then go away and leave the stunts to us."

The finished film demands that it look as if the actor "is doing all the action, but most actors can obviously only take it half way. So he might go half way over a balcony, for example, then the stuntman must take the fall. That is harder to do than take the whole fall, with momentum, over the balcony."

Paul Weston did not have one day off during the entire shoot of Robin Hood, because of its frantic pace. On the occasional clear Sunday, he was either travelling to the next location or setting up the next stunt.

and with Mel Gibson in *Air America* (1990).

In truth, he says, the fear is always there. But there were two particular sequences in the all-action *Robin Hood* which brought him a special edge of danger.

"The first was in the big battle scene in Robin's camp, which involved diving from one tree house to another - and the rope breaks. Robin falls and you don't know whether he is dead or alive. The main problem in that was that our rope is 12 feet away from the first tree house. I had to run and dive from the house onto the rope, which gives you a very big jolt as you start to swing along. It was a 60-feet fall and the rope was on fire. I had to be careful that it did not fall on me - and that I fell in the correct landing - an air bag covered in tarpaulin, to make it look like a small hut.

"On one of the takes my hands slipped from the rope and I fell on to the air bag. We did it successfully and safely, of course, but that needed a lot of careful preparation.

"The second most difficult sequence is when Robin is trying to rescue Marian from her marriage to the Sheriff. He is running along the castle roof top, jumping from one stone to another. He grabs hold of a banner, jumps from the castle and swings down through a window using the banner as a rope. It was a tough one to do.

"Half the sequence had to be filmed in a castle in France. But I obviously could not go crashing through a window there so we used a crash pad on the wall, about 12 inches thick. I thumped against that a few times in the takes and did the second half of the window sequence back at Shepperton Studios, using 'toffee glass' instead of real glass.

"To do those two sequences successfully gave me the most satisfaction."

Simon genuinely admired Costner for his insistence on doing as much action as possible: "I consider that my job is to make the stunt safe - and make him look good," he says. "The only thing I wore to match his appearance was a wig. The rest is down to acting: watching how he walks, runs and moves. I would watch him act on set and look for certain points to follow."

Archery Expert

Archery expert GABE CRONNELLY was chosen to perform all the key shooting scenes which required a high standard of accuracy. As ever with filming, a top quality performance was needed for take after take.

His most difficult task was splitting the hangman's noose as Robin attempts to rescue his woodsmen from the Sheriff's gallows.

"Robin might have just done it at 50 yards distance if he used a broadhead arrow - and was very lucky," he says. "But I needed spot-on accuracy. So I was in a kneeling position so I would not be seen on camera, about seven or eight yards from the rope, using a modern compound bow. Fortunately, we only needed two takes and I split the rope on both occasions."

For the remainder of the film, though, Gabe used the authentic yew bows crafted especially for the film: "They were extremely deadly," he reports. "At 250 yards it is possible to accurately shoot an arrow into the space of a small garden and at 40 yards you can pick off any target.

"In Robin's day they would occasionally use what are called Bodkin Piles as arrow-heads, which could penetrate armour one-eighth of an inch thick at 200 yards. The same arrow over the same distance would penetrate solid oak by four inches. An arrow has a soaring movement in the air and accuracy would have been incredible.

"Archers were brought up to the use of the bow from childhood. The bow-makers, arrow-makers and fletchers, who added the feathers, were highly sophisticated. And the archers were far more accurate with a long-bow than a trained archer today. The art was passed on from generation to generation.

"They would use about 12 different woods in the making of the arrows, for example - ash was the favourite - and would fletch them differently for each sort of weather condition. Young goose feathers were fletched on to an arrow for use on a fine day; old feathers, which were stiffer, were used for windy days.

"We have to remember that the bow and arrow was used for catching food, for protection and for war. It was vital to have first-class men trained to use them."

Gabe, in much demand as a stunt man over the years in

films like *Superman* and *Indiana Jones and the Last Crusade* (1990), is one of the recognized archery experts in the United Kingdom. He has represented his native Ireland in archery events many times at international level and has a degree in history, his speciality being Medieval History.

OPPOSITE TOP : *Robin and Azeem fire from the battlements.*
BELOW: *The woodsmen form a defensive line, bows at the ready.*
BOTTOM LEFT: *Robin loosens an arrow.*

"I was always fascinated by the historical fact that at the Battle of Agincourt in 1415 (approximately 150 to 200 years after Robin Hood, depending on which research is accepted) when the English fought the French, it was the heavily outnumbered English archers who won the day," he says. There were 7,000 of them, against 45,000 Frenchmen. Three hours later they had killed 10,000 against just 300 casualties of their own and the battle was won. "It gives you an idea of just how lethal a bow and arrow was, if used in the right way."

CREDITS

CAST LIST

Robin of Locksley	KEVIN COSTNER	John Little	NICK BRIMBLE
Azeem	MORGAN FREEMAN	Fanny	SOO DROUET
Will Scarlett	CHRISTIAN SLATER	Wulf	DANIEL NEWMAN
Sheriff of Nottingham	ALAN RICKMAN	Bull	DANIEL PEACOCK
Marian	MARY ELIZABETH MASTRANTONIO	Duncan	WALTER SPARROW
Mortianna	GERALDINE MCEWAN	Bishop of Hereford	HAROLD INNOCENT
Friar Tuck	MICHEAL MCSHANE	Much	JACK WILD
Lord Locksley	BRIAN BLESSED	Kenneth of Cowfall	MICHAEL GOLDIE
Guy of Gisborne	MICHAEL WINCOTT	Peter Dubois	LIAM HALLIGAN

UNIT LIST

EXECUTIVE PRODUCER	James G. Robinson	EDITOR	Peter Boyle
EXECUTIVE CO-PRODUCERS	David Nicksay & Gary Barber	COSTUME DESIGNER	John Bloomfield
DIRECTOR	Kevin Reynolds	CASTING DIRECTORS	Noel Davis, Jeremy Zimmerman (U.K.)
PRODUCERS	John Watson, Pen Densham and Richard B. Lewis		Ilene Starger (U.S.)
CO-PRODUCER	Michael J. Kagan	SPECIAL EFFECTS SUPERVISOR	John Evans
STORY BY	Pen Densham	STUNT CO-ORDINATOR	Paul Weston
SCREENPLAY	Pen Densham & John Watson	STILLS PHOTOGRAPHER	David James
MUSIC BY	Michael Kamen	SPECIAL PUBLICITY	Ronni Chasen
DIRECTOR OF PHOTOGRAPHY	Douglas Milsome, B.S.C.	SECOND UNIT DIRECTORS	Mark Illsley, Max J. Kleve
PRODUCTION DESIGNER	John Graysmark	PRODUCTION SUPERVISOR	Malcolm Christopher
SET DECORATOR	Peter Young	ARCHERY EXPERT	Gabe Cronnelly
		STUNT DOUBLE	Simon Crane

(CREDITS NOT CONTRACTUAL)

ACKNOWLEDGMENTS

The publishers would like to thank the following organisations for their kind permission to reproduce the photographs in this book:

All photographs copyright MORGAN CREEK PRODUCTIONS, INC.

except: The Ronald Grant Archive/Exclusive Films 12 top; /United Artists 10 top; /by courtesy of Warner Bros. Inc. 13 top;

The Kobal Collection/by courtesy of Columbia Pictures Industries Inc. 11, 12 bottom, 13 bottom;

/by courtesy of Warner Bros. Inc. 10 centre, bottom left and bottom right.